Along a Ruined Sea

by Larry Kuechlin

Alabaster & Mercury
Ocean Beach, California

Kuechlin, Larry
Along a Ruined Sea; p. cm
ISBN-13: 978-0-9822591-4-6 (paper : alk. paper)
ISBN-10: 098225914X (paper : alk. paper)
Copyright © 2008 by Larry L. Kuechlin, Jr.
Library of Congress Number: TX0007158011

Second Edition.

All rights reserved. Printed in the United States of America. No part of this book may be used or reproduced in any manner whatsoever without the express written permission except in the case of brief quotations embodied in critical articles and reviews.

Published by:
Alabaster & Mercury
Ocean Beach, California, USA

Many of these poems were previously published in periodicals.

This book was originally published in 2008 by d/e/a/d/b/e/a/t/ Publishing; editor, Jack Henry: and then published in a special edition by Avalon Press; editor Susan Glover. I want to express my sincere thanks to both of these fine publishing houses and editors for taking my work into their hearts as their own.

As much as possible, I have left the order of the original book as Jack Henry laid it out, but I have added some poems that were supposed to go in a follow up book that never happened. The two poems, "Cathedral" and "Red Devil Inn" belong in this collection because my voice changed significantly after this came out.

Also from Larry Kuechlin:

Mountain Biking Orange County
Randy Vogel and Larry Kuechlin, Globe Pequot Press

Along a Ruined Sea
d/e/a/d/b/e/a/t/ Publishing (2008)

Along a Ruined Sea: Special Edition
Avalon Press (2010)
Nominated for the Kate Tufts Discovery Award

Entrances: 30 Poems and 100 Lines About Love
Avalon Press (2011)

Something Still Visible In the Fire
Alabaster & Mercury, 2012
Nominated for the Pushcart Prize for Poetry

elemental
Alabaster & Mercury, 2012
Nominated for the Kingsley Tufts Poetry Award & the Pushcart Prize for Poetry

the Falling Place
Alabaster & Mercury, 2013

for William Kuechlin and Ruth Wilkinson

Introduction

When I was asked to write the introduction to Larry Kuechlin's first volume of poetry, I was delighted. For the year or so that I have known him, I cannot think of anyone I have given a harder time to or teased more. The chance to ruin the introduction to his book was irresistible.

Firstly, if you are a woman, just put the book down and walk away. I have no idea why, but he seems to have this effect on women: they swoon and sigh and fall a little bit more in love with him with each poem they read.

Don't put yourself through this. Just throw the book away now.

To best explain how good a poet I think Larry is, and how nasty I have been to him, I'll share one of the cruel tricks I tried to play on him. We have a game in which someone gives a title and the recipient has to try to make a poem from the subject as quickly as possible. The very first title I gave Larry was "The secret diary of Charles Dickens – his cross-dressing crack-abuse phase". Larry came up with a poem I think is tremendous, "Charles in the Park". Anyone else would have told me where to go.

Larry has a style and voice that are all his own. That is rare, indeed. You can trace where it came from, and the poets he read to get there, but it is all his and it's a voice I adore.

What you will learn from reading these is how easy it is to feel that you know Larry. By the end of the book I am sure you will think of him as a friend, and if you let yourself be immersed in the poetry, then he will be. I don't know what you want from poetry, but I want heart, thought, beauty, accessibility and more heart. Larry delivers.

He is six foot infinity tall, and the sort of person you want on your side when you are in a tight corner.

He is also a complete numpty.

Oh and he surfs.

I love him.

Si Philbrook
Poet

Of Pen and Ink

04: Dedication & Introduction by Si Philbrook
06: Contents
08: Forward, *Manifesto*

Poetry

10: Travelin'
14: Of Water
15: Ice Skating
18: Against the Rain
19: Viewpoint
22: the Forgetting Tree
26: Ring
27: Cathedral
30: Café Reading
33: Hurricane, Utah
36: Sonnets and Unrealities
37: A Fisherman's Hands
40: Brick Upon Brick
44: Impressions
46: Alfonsina's
48: Adagio
50: the Kid
54: Fort Rosecrans
56: Driftingly
58: Charles In the Park
60: Love Song for Nobody
62: Through My Window
64: Consequence
66: Angels and Iris
67: Red Devil Inn
72: Lloyd
74: Seattle, Barwise
76: Quetzalcoatl

78: Simple Words
80: A Dance Beneath Scars
81: Window
84: Canticle
86: Psalms
90: I Turned

Prose

094: Convenience Store Burritos
100: Days Like These
108: Crazy Walking Dude

About the Author

Manifesto

The danger of Irises
is beautifully
pallid;

they cannot be unseen:

a failure
upon which
to measure your

striving.

You read my words
but do you hear me?

I would burn every poem
I have ever written
to hold someone's hand
for a single day

as if they meant it.

Travelin'

for Si Philbrook

My soul has grown deep like the rivers...

The River never ends:

it just shades away
under a Cajun drawl
of cypress trees
and back water deltas.
It whispers you tired...

Come see...

the history in my silt,
the souls in my draw;
the story of My every shame
floating the trash
of my decayed canals:

but these are my waters,
Choctaw waters.

The fingers of a nation
trying to hold
what has washed long away.
America...her dreams;
languid in the silt of her
terrible scars and hidden bones
layin' down shadow slow
to the Gulf.

On the Plaquamine Locks;

the Schwing Mill long
down broke in rusted clarity:
walking just to get the
walkin' out.

The River is here and
the water gloams me near.

The barges glide;
air horns weep their souls into
a tangle of willow and cotton wood.
I am breathing just to
feel alive.

Tumbled towards the edge;
towards the River
and my never knowing.
I wipe my eyes quick:
the River…I should
never leave but always do.

An old black man holds a guitar
forlorn in the settling dark;
sittin' in the cypress knees.
I listen to him scratch and scat

Gotta keep movin'
Gotta keep movin'
Blues fallin down like hail…

Hell Hound On My Trail;
hammers the G with velvet.
I watch him 7 frets into a 9 fret cord:

Nobody played like Robert… 'spect no one ever will.

    How did you…?

Your eyes, son. You know Robert. You travelin'?

I'm here on business.

*Not what I asked t'all
but I 'spect you know that.
You're travelin' to find your waters, son
and the River…it don't ever sleep.*

*No sir, it doesn't. The River? Hell,
my soul is deep like the River.*

*Langston would have liked you, son.
Yeah, he was my friend.
You spend time by the River…
everyone floats by.*

I smile, and walk
crossroads away.
His music fades
into my any imagining.

The evening hangs her
magenta in raven hair;
his cords progress into
a cypress echo.
Dragonflies skip their gems
across a hush of River;
sapphires and emeralds
lilting a fais-do-do
into a sway of
Spanish moss moon.

I smell chicory and
tomorrow's beignets
and I am blackberry dreaming
of brambled back roads
along our every excess.

Heat glowers the Gulf;
sets a hyacinth
in the mouth of

an angry Stream;
darkness will have
magnolia scars as

our deepest heart utters
its angry judgments:

beauty and death
mournful in the
currents of time;
and We are just that;

travelin' to the Delta,
soothed along the Lun de Lac;
curved and closing;
and jazz, it does swoon
evening slumber
into reed-restless cerulean:

America;

moment by day
recedes into the
slowly sea.

Of Water

Above the Canyon, and long with me, you
lie under the voice of Talking God. Our
sky drifts down a unison of souls to
soft ruin. I am so weary in this hour,

weary in the steps of my Fathers. *O!*
My heart; I have never been of these words!
I am of water; a life in the flow
along Anasazi canyons, seaward

down the San Juan as night paints an indigo
pony, roan deep to calico: a burl
among quiet cedars. My eyes; so slow:
our fire flickers to fade, as smoke curls

the rise of final hands to prayerful rain;
the earth rising up; blood of my blood again.

Ice Skating

I come here for the coffee,

ice and darkness;
a drown of some comfort.
Alone with the sounds of
ice against the blade;
words rushing by;
shrieks; suddenly and gone;
coaches extol the
virtues of axles and steady
revolutions;
training kids for an event
they will never attend;
deepening the shine
of their often eyes, for naught:
practicing how to be

beautiful.

Corpulent words are bantered by
self important guardians:

> *Meredith's mini-van*
> *dropped the tranny…*
> *fucking American cars!*
> *Coach what's-his-name*
> *is such an asshole!*
> *Can you believe he didn't like*
> *little Daniele's routine?*

These words pass over me;
glacial; reminiscent but
cold…long dead.

They notice me, but
never ask why:

        why I sit on the top bleacher;
        why I look so often away;
        why I talk to myself;

to you.

    Help me remember…

this prayer I recite
for all those things
you let slip away with
only a kiss of a promise
you'll write them all

stone down;
they forget their way
back to me now;
the trauma chasing them
so very dark…

lost;
the sounds of your sleep;
                 there,

on the pillow with
the still impression of
your dreaming;
its music and hush;

just there

in the brush of linger
where breath
is only a slight notion
between desires:

unimportant things

that make a home
more than a collection of
preferable debris;
keepsakes of dimly time
that hold me cold
drinking black coffee
here in the quite of ice.

    I hate their fucking coffee.

I huddle against

    my dark;
    my cold;

let my mind axle and revolve;
ice against the blade;
practicing something
I will never again

be.

Against the Rain

A truth of emotion, this simple act;
whispered to you against a drown of sky;
I love you. I wish I could take them back;
snatch each word, like ravens against my night;

put them back to breath and hidden pages;
unconfer again this confession born
of anguish; spoken when the night rages
alone against my heart. Each sound torn

from our unfolding; this friendship I hold
with hands that cannot lift the light of stars
back into my own eyes. These words I told
you; the place you keep in my life; so far

from the awkward notes I have sung into
the silence between words we both unsay;
a buttress against our breaking. Please, will you
speak to me just now, dear friend, that I may

listen to your voice, long against the rain;
hear your beautiful heart; and tell you once again.

Viewpoint

I am flawed;

broken in ways that are contained in a
larger breaking.

I see the world wrong.

I see the world
dimensional as death;
stoic streams of
color in the rust;
a naiveté of dust and tumble
assessing beauty
amidst the squalor.

I am third-world conversant;

but I see a child;
Mexicali farm girl sing clap dancing;
poor as stones that shall never be bread,
and my heart is filled

only with

a little girl, smudged
in her violet vagaries; beauty
perfected in the squalor;
pristine of light
flared into my lens;
resplendent in the
red clay of her fields;

porcelain precious;

sung of stars that longingly lullaby her,

fairy tale away;

> *not the macro-economic*
> *struggle against neo-con forces*
> *that endeavour to illegally*
> *starve democracies and*
> *the will of dire masses*
> *from their God (or ungod) given,*
> *rightful place; a move towards*
> *enlightened society: replete with*

Brittney Spears custody dramas and
Jerry Springer toothless unrealities.

I see only

a most wonderful life
lived by Jose Morales;
a man with nothing but everything;
alive upon the Sea of Cortez; a man
rough of hands and means;
loved and loving;
happy upon his dirt floor.

No complaints of Cortez and his atrocities.
No complaints of whichever government
resides incompetently in Mexico City.

He is across the farther Sea
and birds are working
their heavenly magic
as he plies his trade
across the gold
Cortez left behind;

and there is always joy
in his homeward song
as he angles his eyes
across the panga, heavy
with an honest days work;

a life perfectly wrought;

and I am broken just this way:

broken to see the beauty
and love the people
and not worry about

a why

that is far too late for me to change.
I am broken as the breaking of bread;
as the refraction of hope
into a Baja shadow.

Love; love

is all that matters;
it is all I have;
it is all I can see;

and I am flawed
with it.

the Forgetting Tree

I left the invitation unopened.

It was unnecessary;
all these years later
I knew where to
find you.

I walked the paths
of Old Town Sacramento;

stones covered in
the grey of time;
walked along the
gas lamps and
café's as they
breathed their jazz
into the Delta heat;

walked up the bluff
along the tired water
of the Sacramento River
to the magnolia tree
your father planted
for you.

I found you there;

staring up into the tree
you loved;
a great expanse of
blossoms and branches
that filled your eyes:
I called out to you
but you would not speak;

ran my fingers through
the ravens of your hair;

and still you would not speak;

touched you where just
your heart is hewn rough;

followed it to blood;
followed it
until the smooth lines
of your life were
stone apparent; and
still

you would not speak to me
there, under the great tree
planted to keep you from
running to sky.

A father's wish.

I took the last pull
from our bottle of Gold
and dropped it next to you
in the dirt under

the Forgetting Tree.

I walked the hush
of half dark;
the last glint of a day
desperate to remember

light;

along the slowly
Sacramento,
whispered Delta
down the river

where I can
see your eyes
aflame in magnolia;
see your lips
drifting towards me in

snowflakes and silences;

see you sitting where
love is still

beautiful;

on my bed; bouquet
across your smile;
but I could not
remember

your voice.

The yellowed parchment
tumbled in my hands
to red, as I watched
the swallows
sway night;

carry the Sacramento
homeward, gem
by drop;

heard the sonata
of cattails and wind
over the old prayer of River
sliding ocean away.

And in the
great arch of

the Forgetting Tree,

I heard
the starlings
sing the stars to
shine;
turned my eyes to blue
and smiled:

    Thank you.

Ring

The rain came;
window down a morning gleam;

radio wave starshine
intimated into my directly
dreaming; words glanced
between nuzzled eyes
and breath;

placed in pieces
whorl by wisp:
and I was eternal in
a canvas of you.

Am I supposed to
drift, dawning back,
before the fractal moment?
Am I rain in the peek
of open window?

The wind rushing seawards past
holds no reply in the hurry;
clouds cannot be reset
desire by drop into the raging;

rain runs to the always sea,
and settles deeply;

as do I.

Cathedral

The White Mountains are
gliding gone.

It never snows in September...

I watch the Carson Valley Plain,
broken as sky and
                           falling;
  torn as thunder.

The Owens River gleams a frostshine now;

a bitter light, dying a
lingered sway to salt
               as Death Valley
shines a close horizon.

      I am standing with you;
      I am always standing with you

here in the spires and tumble;
a place to find death or
      lasting reality;
larger than these frail gods
we cower before:

      The American West at 11, 000 feet;

rust in the air-thin toil and
vividly breathing:
a place to break your
living or your life;
Freedom, the way we no longer remember.

      Storm's comin'...you think we should go?

I look valley down The Eastern Sierras,
down Heartbreak Ridge.
Jagged is perfectly placed
upon this granite;

        a cathedral

of course solitude and
reflective fracture.

Blue Lake draws an alpine breath;
azure brilliance in the disappear…
                bruised in the roil;
dying a slow gold
   upon winter stone white.

The Dogwoods bend a reverent strain
but stand borealis tall.

Sound is lost here;
the world wanders a
conflux of keen listening
              and windrush.

On the ridge
 snow clouds us deaf and low;
  so slight and heavy above our heads.
            You reach up your hand and
snatch dreamshine
         angel down.

We speak in glances and light;
my answer, so very slow in the fall…

our campfire dances red mischief,
cluttered in blue enamel and
strong coffee;

        the Indian way of heat;

flame small and heart close.

Always, I am next to you;
Always, I…

The burn cracks White Pine
into the moment and
you lay your shoulder to mine;

        our hands

silent on the warm;
wool gloves, hiding Heaven to curl

a Loon holds far sway across
                    the claire de lune

a Titmouse sings her ruffled slumber

Blue Lake is autumn deep and
drifting ideas of softly time;

song quiet in the
                  hush
these quiet things that
          flicker in the
pass of sighs,

      white held

in close

fire.

Café Reading

for Beth Turner

Jungle Java always has light
dancing in the proper amounts,
and boisterous clutter
to adequately hide:

it's my forever choice.

Paula runs the place
brightly in her
coyless laughter;
the fussing of milk
and frothing steam
cannot hide
the sounds of her shining:
darkly haired and deeply eyed…
gauze skirts and
the teaseful lilt of
olive curves
under shouldered barely T's:

ocean wrought beauty.

He stands
uneasily angled in his
tauntingly draped
youthfulness:

hides in the crowd
like August sunlight;
carouses drunkenly
into a fragile morning.
He smiles the stars of
all immense gods.

Their eyes
······touch
······retreat
······touch…
hummingbirds;
nectar drunk in their
sudden alighting.

He sits with his coffee and
turns a glance over his quick pages.

I order;

the light of her
fills my chest
as I breathe her
every jasmine.

······*Cummings? Are you a student?*

I smile deeply down
from my any shy ringing.
The tip conveys the answer.

······*No…but I'm always learning.*

I fumble back into
the tatters of my joy-spun hiding.

the emperor…

How many times have I read this?
I smile to nobody in particular.

Prufrock, Fern Hill, In My Craft Or Sullen Art?

Dear, old friends; all.

The Java god smiles,
beckoning with eyeful sun.

The pages
turn bright
under his
intently gazing:

Harry Potter and the Deathly Hallows.
Paula looks
glancingly into him.

I take a
last sighful linger
towards the
flowers of her light
and disappear
into the always arms
of my good friends.

The settling of tea cups
draws me moonshine back:

    Would you read me your favorite?

Hurricane, Utah

The tail lights grow
pavement thin across
this fine line moon
and the mesas hold the night
close to their impossibly
brittle wind;
branches in a
tease of dancing flame
and suddenly
diesel lingered light.

August.

Male rain has run
through its anger
and left the sky
a roiling cobalt
and cloud.

The trucks flash their
sleeping trims in
their running darkness;
and I am lot bound;
watching the slow drag
of glowing reservation smokes.

The Big H Truck Stop

My heart can see an America
stark in blue black
luminescence.

The drivers jest…
they laugh from their cabs
drunken in their

intentful raging.

While Shoshone girls
starlit wander Route 85
where Pintos
and warriors once ran:
calico Cochinas
chambray pressed and
sun dancingly pleated;
braids black and strong
waving an unwinded unison
in their laughing
unquiet arms.

Mother astride
in her white and black
Big H uniform;
walking past the
Indian Cultural Center:
explaining no culture
known to an Indian

or standing Warrior.

The Peterbilt wavers onto
the shoulder...
puddle mud;

this derisive rain
covers the
first residents of this
place of windful time.

The Shoshone walk on,
dripping in their pride;
alone in their muddied
eternal

knowing.

The Peterbilt
gives two long tones
from an air haughty
horn.
The wind washes still;
it howls down a
pride cut,
longingly ancient
canyon.

And nightfully delicate
Shoshone girls
pray their lives
into an

always touching wind.

Sonnets and Unrealities

You)
diffuse a shine of satellite spun
night; this depleted reasoning of dark;
a falchion shear of eyewardly held burn

and light. These waves,

cold cast and stark,
ring the garnet of our laughter and wine;
these brush strokes, impressionistic
of swoon; traced, flame to silk
along your curve

and wane; this touch,

that fractures our separate moons;
which, before your voice,
stand sapphire to gleam;

this ocean which drowns the starlight deepest.
I should dance down every heaven to dream,
than angel one violet frail for harvest

; but for you; just;

I will sin these rules, to be known
in a heart, sun-iris wild

amongst all fire grown.(

A Fisherman's Hands

The Sea of Cortez
holds no keepsakes
in the bleach and bone.

I walk the hour of wings
when the gloam of you
sings the wind to silk
under this empyrean wheel
of heaven to white;
cast my net upon
umber and shine
with hands cut
rough to salt;

and you are softer than moonlight.

And in the fleeting,
snow wavers dream jade
under an egrets gaze,
as Frigates spire the
dark drifts of flame,
and avocets stride the dying

fire.

At the market
once, I saw you
across the call of merchants;
and you stood silent
against a sky,
buckled under your
grace, and drifted so.

And I thought,
just once,

I could touch you;
I could reach into
your smile

and touch you where
the light of you
would not be worn away
under the rough
ends of my days, and

your eyes
would hold me

just once,

precious
in those seconds

before life
washed back over
your sight;

but you were gone.

And in this hour
I cast a tired net,
as my hands
fall oceans deep
upon the waters of
Cortez;

still

I see you

through clenched eyes
and dreaming; clearly
in the tides that run
black and light;

I leave my life
strewn towards you
in the sands
along a ruined sea
when just

fire lays upon gold,

and lament the moon
among many birds.

Brick Upon Brick

You are always
(in my eyes) there:

work worn in your overalls;
transient among gardenias and
apple reds; boughed as laughter,
fallen as chestnut strayed
across your eyes; shining
eternity upon perennials

; we

(wildflowered, a
forward supposition)

build our garden
brick upon brick.
You spade the loam,
dig to the deeper
a futility of containment
this cataclysm of
hued living;

vines our only vanity; we
wrangle the technicolor
with wilding eyes
and dreaming in this, our
sacrament of sanctuary;

for gardens harbor wild ideas;

subtle reformation of
needs and desires; of
life loosely burning;
adjustments; slight above

our luminations;
solidly ephemeral; bricks without
the stiffness of mortar;
flux flagrant;
expansive into blossomed
wildernesses, yet tendriled.

You walk the rows;
flower upon your
flowers;
spade; comically abrupt
into the tall shade;
under the figs of your being;
larger than your leaning

and I can only see you this way;
in the mayhem of
marigolds and poppies;
paint splotched;
one strap coylessly askew;
draped of evening pears
air pungent and salt kissed
in this sea wrought breeze.
Just you, reflective in
resplendence,
upon the sitting bench
in our garden, nestled; laden
with sounds of oak curving
into your

      vivacious Joy;

as a slithered Jewel;
serpentine into our ruby ruminations;
shows slowly a brash blaze;
and hovers in our genesis of cultivation.

Heavenly opened…

drops and

drop

drop drop
drop

bruising the moment, satin
to somnolence;
fills the lacquered tray: rain,
ocean born and warm
diluted delicious into
chilled green tea and mangos,
cut and unashamedly
ripened.
As our magenta becomes
evening, impatient in the roil:
Blossom is shouting about,
tail spun and run jumping
over our garden; barking,
dance desperate for understanding;
Cockatoos, wild and concupiscent
among the almonds

(black plumed and diffident of daffodils)

crow a raucous debate;
and the Jewel coil-slithers
to more refined environs
beneath topaz sated sunflowers;
and tulips turn a concerned
face towards your shining
as the wind blows your
laughter over my softly eyes
and you stand with your
spade, hopelessly asunder
between the touch tap of sky
burgeoning upon us,
down and spring suddenly falling,

and I have forgotten how

to stop kissing so impossibly
you.

Silence; and your always smile.

I take slowly your hand
as you glide afternoon
away, drifting our daylight
gardenia down,

I: no;

wait, please just now;
(between the exhale of
indigo and my any fears) which,
tremulous before this silence
streams downpour
away; please,

just now;

    I must tell you:

Impressions

Where upon,

the lingering of
your suddenly head settled,
is bruised as still singing;

(which, into
my careless beating,
sprang fountains
unspeakable as flowers;
upturned in their very
topaz hungry
faces.)

And lavished
by a momentary touch
into your uncautiously
awakening;

frail upon my
constantly lips

your saffron sordidly
imaginings
become fleshly
forgotten as
translucent heaven:
and alabaster does
quake in the tumult
of your blazingly always

violets.
And,
should I,
among all honey,

thrumming like the
madly sun
lay you so driftingly
down
where spring is
clumsily aflame
and rowdy among
the tulips;
and put the
kiss on the clover
up so floatingly dreamward
to dance the
fire awry.

We are,
from a considerable
red impression pulled
splendored down
for time
and dizzily time;
lost among
a brightly breathing

while jasmine pours its course
through mingled
hands.

Alfonsina's

You taste the desert before
you actually see it;
a smell of old life turning bad
under cloud-dry blue.

You weep moon dust
and barely-burning gas;
the hulking rust of hopeful abandon
lies tumbled in the creosote
and jar-tooth washboard.

Time is a lost arrow these days;
swerved and avoided

forever rutted along
tire-tread horizons and alluvion sand.

Life here is a kicked-can
broken axle, a forlorn print
of all passing souls
never washed away;

a sliver of sapphire
bumping over the dashboard
fertile of windshield cracks
and imagined hope.

Pleated girls wait

in the little white they have
jostling, arms dancing;
at the only crossroad to Alfonsina's.

Pemex will be there someday.
They hold their lives

in folded paper sacks;
pigtails swaying in
morning laughter.

The bus will not come
today, but still they wait.

Baja is a life-shine;
deep breaths in the devil dust

of always patient
rusting.

Adagio

That is why I am on this porch...

Weaving the bight
silent in stride,
the avocet flees the gossip of
sun-shell afternoons

in the rush of shore;

wavered of sea grass
and the still of gliding Leopards.

Tangled of arm and drift,
we recede the held heart
and sun the shoulder
of scent: honeysuckle;
wild as bees,

        hunt hunt;
        fly the vine

of summer thorn;
and close the lamp on dark waters.

The quay sleeps the song of sway and wood,
bone of last years brush:

        Requiescat in pace.

        White,
        white hands

ring the indigo of alabaster music,
wont of mercury and muse;
adagio and sea.

We sing the salt of avocet cry,
and drink the breath of familiar voices:

spirits sharing a hint of heaven passing
the unspace between,

as we walk the stones of Peter, torn of tides:

so deep the drown of crossing waters.

In the hush of sliding sea,
the still cry of avocet
pools a call of long water,
close of gathered distance
and the seaward

reach of hands

towards a faith so slight of shadow.

And I word the breath of night
to wet her mouth of ocean fire,

lit in the flotsam crook
of our cluttered secrets:
fallen to arms of Siren's quick
and the call to blind rock.

Walking these whispered stones;
blanch under strings of star;
we dance the wing of darkness drawing:

our spindrift sighs,
soft in tumbled hands,
gales the pull of
parried night;

and everywhere,
the crush of moon.

the Kid

And he carries a reminder…

He walks his unquiet nightmares
along the black dead edges
of solo riffs and spotlights
with Danny, Eddie and Eric:
fingers roiling the air
the heat of solo riffs
that flow fast
to the gathered back turn;
playing the crowded alleyways
in the limelight of
suburban bustle
and delivery trucks;
he burns and wails
against a stucco backdrop:

the Apple Tree Kid;

he leaves no open case…
plays for the music,

    Man, it's all about the music…

Walkman taped in
6 places.

Never makes a sound.

His every spoken anguish
is in his music;

    Man, it's all about the music…

and we watch him
with the shuffled eyes
of rushing feet;
pass him dark sky over
this parody of life;
a fire-born disease
that may never be cleansed.

One though, she shuffle runs away
and drops her icon at his feet:

   'ady…'ady….your 'allet…'ALLET!

she runs
she throws her bags in the car
the Kid stands;
one hand lonely

out

   'ady…

but the demons win.
He drops death down
into a raging twist
and she screams into her
shiny retreat and howls away.

And the Kid lies

shuffled among the every
quick feet;
a torn image
of his forlorn façade;
limbs jerking, head tossing
neck askew:

bleeding onto the scattered path
of the ungathered shun:

fighting the evil in his code.

And I run to him from
another world.

The Apple Tree is graced again;
the Kid holds court
with the Masters;
scabs on his elbows and cheek;
hair matted down;

his Van Halen shirt
streaked and torn;

another piece of tape on
the backdrop of his life.
And I dig deep
for the loose change
of our pocketed souls as
the Kid wails:

back turned
arching in the riffs
running the board;
hammering his vivid seeing
echo away;

chasing the shadows
note by note;

    Man, it's all about…

God, I want that kind of love;
I look long for it
into the convulsive corners of
my own unseeing.

I search the lost light
of my shattered down heart
for his

wail and soul;

deeper than spurned
madness;
deep into the
luminous mind
of his always

unmaligned dancing,

and the shadow boxing
of elusive daemon rages:
just to once know
the burst shine of his
very angeled stars
and the noteful
tempting of all

weeping heaven.

> *Man, it's all about the*
>
> *music.*

Fort Rosecrans

Along the fields
of crocus and karst,
above calling ocean
and the mournful whisper
of shores
drawn slowly away,
I pass, a stranger
among brothers
on their keepful watch
of untold honor.

Abandoned centuries past,
together they stand,
eternal in the breach
of silent vigilance
with arms strong of stone
and valor.

Above this sanctuary

of whitened sea
I pass; a stranger
awash in private pain
and the burnished bouquets
of forlorn remembrances.

Her faltering angel,
left behind long alone,
fails once more
her need to be
upward born,

so she falls upon
these forgotten fields,
foreign only to the living:

      a wife
      a mother
      a languished love lost;

the hand of wavering alabaster
and reaching tears
entreats torn towards the
shoulders worn heaven away:
knelt so deeply
she will never

rise again.

Driftingly

driftingly

(always
I must tell you now)

I found, and
frail,

these 3 words;

intoxicants amongst a comet's burn;
immersed in your uncautiously
                                laughter.

And dancing upon the
edge of scattered sea; this

delight;

where certain twilights are found
kissing; haphazardly under the shine of
curtains drawn;
        precisely pearled and
jewelled downward; seeing them,

these 3,
in casual clarity…O
look, the very
world.

I picked them up
as a tumble of swallows
will snatch an opal
from a glint of just windily evening.

And I,
thinking upon
the wildflowers of
such words
(and since dreams are
fussing,
starrily about)
thought,

perhaps,

I could,
where carefully your lips
curl the sun of
my indecently smiling;
pour the covey of them
slow flowing
upon your softly neck
and sway;
where the music of us

joyously burns

and I can feel the hush of you
decadently upon my desires;

where,
upon you; and
towards your
very heart, I
will sing them
rhapsody away and

whispered
into cerulean octaves
measured only in

angels.

Charles In the Park

for Si Philbrook

The magnolias
are ringing in the heat
and I am burning
a sloe,
sloe afternoon
down a dying cup.
I'm a "writer"
so I simply
must attend.

Keep up appearances whatever you do…

The women
bounce and banter
about progeny and
stitching
and just the right
shade of eyeliner:
delivered in their opulence
to this home of lost souls
and terminally
forgotten.

A smattering of everything…

There is dawning attention
ginned up
towards my shadow.

What do you think?

The dying ring of their banter
flies suicidal off the bluff.

Dickens was gay, you know.

Tale of Two Cities?
An allegory for sex.
Written in prison
about the two men
fighting over him.

He only wore the finest dresses
I'm told.

    A knowledge of nothing…

The magnolias ring
over the long grass;
women fade white and go;
heads turned down,
farthest down,
till they see the tattered,
sleeping in the corners; and
their opulence seems
shiny as a

dead man's penny.

Love Song For Nobody

for Alba

A kiss is just that,
which upon
unknowing Spring,
all burning green
entwines wildflowered
into delightful
madness; and
the laughing emerald
of your persistent glances,
alights cartwheeled marvelous
upon any impetuous petal
drifting soulward
before our honey scattered
hearts.

A moon is just that,
which upon a
drunken shore
bows its white mischief
onto our sea pale feet,
and temptfully throws
pearls and naked rubies
upon the muses
dancing gold towards
our always touching eyes:
which upon the
wandering off,
all ocean vagaries
lingers us softly
into a sapphire delicious
undarkness.

A

you and I

is just that
which upon any sky
learned its
songbird suddenly
magic
and every whirl-tilt
heaven
fell seraphim away
to the flame of all
persistent gods,
doomed in their
eternal self frailty:

and,

upon which
I only breathe,
and I,

only beating
to no solitary purpose,

drown indigo still into
whisper-star always

you.

Through My Window

Through my window,
the night alights final and glide
over the slump
of broke-back roofs
and ardent wood.
Small in the tucked places,
and lonely among the sills…
the Blackbird sings
the shine on the sun
over the wires that bind,
barbed in black and lilt.
The sinewed scent of Santana
dawns the dance
of fluttered dryads and bright
that cast the colors
over malingered morning.

Through my window
the Blackbird sings…
myriad of meadow;
the shadowed splinter
of tumble-down fences
and the reticent restraints
of ivy edges:
the wraith of echoed allure;
flight and full among
cathedrals of sway
and forgetful ferns:
the prayer of aster oceans
and the brilliant blood
of attar bights.
In the portico places
of private fire
and honeysuckle;
the wreckage of want

and resplendent remains
lift an eye to newer skies,
as through my window
the Blackbird
bows the draw
of pallet and crescendo
to sing the soul of kings
into a wood-worn heart;
shanty and stray.

Consequence

I set my life out
over café linen;
three smooth stones
I have held palm dark
to my heart.

You arrange meaning
to suit your
fears.

      Love with consequence...

Your fingers, slowly
satin in reticence,
trace the stories
of my hands;
scars resting
scimitar strewn
where I have
held life.

      Love with consequence...

You gather me up
fast upon your soothe;
seconds far
across borealis.

My eyes look dark star down.

Your tea cup shines as
jade crosses gold;

you tangle a cool moon
into your hair

and everywhere
raven is set to wing;

fire and raven,

and in your eyes,
a prayer held against
sapphire, sings
our heads bowed
silk slight to
touch; and above,
wisteria conjures
night, pale
into our breath.

Your eyes drown
emerald deep;

    Yes…love with consequence…

Rubies fill the air,
bruised with dancing
as you hold porcelain to

cherry blossom:

I shine the wonder of
which breaking
holds the next

scar.

Angels and Iris

I write poetry because, when sun dark
and madly, I hear only the moon. And yes,
a fool in love with love; this hope-far
beggar of simple things; a stolen kiss

of Coltrane, drowning across a star soaked
drifting; a morning soft smile; a hand I
can only entwine. But I wear a cloak;
a fear of desire, red etched upon my

soul; broken as dreaming; awake as fire.
And upon a mournful verso, I hide
amongst angels and Iris; a ruined prayer
of symbols and saints; impressions of life

that fall upon my heart in Cummings and
Van Gogh: forgive me, this; for I am damned.

Red Devil Inn

Joshua Tree, 1982.

The jagged reach of a wild rough enough
to still be called the West.

       Highway 62 vibrates
with jake brakes and bad retreads.

Life here unfolds like the morning;
far away in a tangle of creosote brambles
as my reality fights off
the exhaustion of a cold mind.

       And I am unsleeping the scene.

It is 28 degrees of desert cold; 6:00 a.m.
I've slept 14 minutes in 14 shifts.

       The Red Devil Inn still has a light on.
       Satan is my salvation this freezing morn.

I enter, disquietly noticed
with the burn of morning at my back;
light doesn't penetrate this place
so much as it avoids it completely.

Lloyd is king of the establishment.
Cancer left him with a hole in his throat.
He smokes Camels through the gap and
billows acrid dying into shadow stale air.

       He has no vocalizer.
He gulps air and burps to speak:

       Who...gulp...are...gulp...you?

Just a climber trying to get out of the cold. Can I get a whisky?

    Well...gulp...mind...gulp...your...gulp...man...gulp...ners.

Whisky appears out of the darkness.
I can see the Keeps hands behind the counter
        but not his arms.
He pours amber from a finger-holed jug.
Not a rocks glass; a tumbler...
        nearly clean.

Straight up.

I drink away
        and let ruined corn warm me towards morning.

There is nothing here
bass-boat Naugahyde and
ad-campaign despair
drifting the beer-stale aura of
        this immovable night.

The pool table is controlled by twin scowls
        and bad advances:
if you squint and turn your head just so,
these two are almost certainly
        not men.
They are not friends:

        brusk in cunning angles of
        bellicose dark;
        short cropped, arm cuffed,
        Harley frayed;
        dive-bar denim chic.

Twitching forearms
tease out and about the table light;
uneasy sticks snap and sway
curling messages of

Lucky Strike dominance
roiled around unfiltered words
that clip the terse silence of any solace.

    Winner buys her the next round....

The contest ensues in a crack.

I watch the hooker.
              Lloyd calls her Shannon.

A pallid hand reaches for her only reality;
the same tumbler, brimmed and amber despondent,
out of her bruised blackness.
Her dress inches towards
destiny and Red regret.
              I can almost see her face:
just a brush of cheek;
alcohol blush on porcelain;
a curve of missing blouse and   forlorn buttons;
full lips, rouged heavily;
she looks of passing street lamps and
                      forgotten desert;
something left to rust into the
      blood red earth.

Her tumbler is nearly drained;
likewise the remaining charity
between the boiling combatants.
With a final crack, the threats
      become imminent reality.

Sticks fly, blood flows.
Lloyd gulps and groans,
his burps are ignored
in equal measure with their
                  adrenaline-soaked pain.

The bar is shattered in their raging
I shade out of sight;

valor is saved for battles worth fighting.

I get to my car and Shannon is there
            waiting for me.
She stands; she shimmers
a dalliance of sun pungent sin;
leans visceral into my closely crimson;
into verified and breath-still me;
inwardly sought and found upon my eyes;
                      touching my cheek:

   Let's get out of here.

Where do you live, darlin?

I turn over the Prelude
and turn east on 62.
        She speaks dreamward subtleties;
        slurs her life to me from a bourbon recoil.
I can hear the desert hush a path
past the fractures of her
            path worn soul.

We drop mile over mile
unnoticed in a ringing of sirocco frost;
Mesquite fingers clatter wild as hooves
windward over unquiet Mormon Tea,
smoothed umber still and final
into a calico mischief
dying the longer hymn of
            the mesa-bound West.

Driving her angels away,
she was my girl; in this,   my reality;
blurred hopelessly along
the receding highway of our dark edges;
jutting angles of Joshua Trees
            into star dazed dark.

We said the goodbyes of strangers,

burning of awkward desires and knowledge
that will remain desert bound and
wandering forgetful Manzanita.
Just then; her face flares into me,
and from a Mojave moon she draws me edgeward…
she tells me those words;
                        the ruby lies
we always need to hear but
run from just as swiftly;
               and we kiss; we kiss
the drown of sudden clarity
under frost lingered light.

She slid my promises and number into her bra
as she slouched through the door.
        I've never been so jealous of paper.
I left under a shine of lunar wane,
and made my way home on bar money
                            without regrets;
the whisky of her deeply on my breath.

       I got a call two days later.

I found her ID that morning:

Shannon Connors; Flagstaff, Arizona;
born, 1966.

I knew who it was.

       Thank you for bringing our daughter home…

Lloyd

for an Ocean Beach Poet

We called after you, Lloyd,
as you drifted down:

I am sure she heard you;

those words
that fell
hollow into the pale;
so very small in their
echo and reach.
I am sure she
saw you there;
under lights placed
poorly against your
ruin;

I am certain she did;

awash in half-dark
and scrapbooked time.
We could hear her
final recede;
see her, oceans afar,
hush the stoop
of your shoulders;

feel her, soft
against your waver;
hearts that
wept in stride, and
slept never apart.

I am sure she heard you;

just then;

your life small sighs
refrained against the cold;
alone with your
creased paper;

draped in worn angels

and faltered silences;
reciting lines
written for your
last shining.

I am sure she heard you

whisper these small matters
you took heavy with you
into a broken night.
Wave upon wave; she

heard you, pray,
tides against your
anguish;

lost along the seawall;
starlit against the crush;
where souls,
deepened in the black,
cling together still;
sinking memory to

madness.

Seattle, Barwise

for Jack Henry

The barwise glitter glides
the black of her dressing dreams
to the corner King,
pocketed in the poetry
of common man;
blood of uncommon song;
prophet of heaven cast burning down.
I am there, in the eternal corner.

She spies the money;
follows the scent;
cleaving another round.
The black dress glides profound
to the rocky Jack, melting shapes
of our bigger dreams:
there's the iconoclast stirring
the dreams of Einstein
in his goblet galaxy
spins the elixir; shins the kick
of narrow masters;
runs the light of longer speed:

the blonde searching the
wrinkles of her laughter;
wholly beautiful;
the Sound under mist,
lilting the look of kindness
in the eye of longer moons:

the songbird of the Locks
and strolled shore;
moon of seaward heart;
tide of haloed soul;
the laughter over lightful love
and starward eternal nova.

The darkened couple;
the laughing silence of she.
Himselves; squeezing the juice
to find the lemon;
out, out the patience
of tumbling hands;
stealing the seal of love
for the passion of shadows.

    The jester;
    the knave;
    the broken,
    dream-small queen;
    the vine-root slave…

and still the King rises
in his riding light and
his always roiling fright.

The separated eyes
of the farther corner,

    bow to his deference;
    bow to his seeing.

Jessica floats the bar
in her cleaving burn
while the King of all the world
beckons; draws the stars
of her light to his eyes;
draws her separation to his till.
She glides; painful in black delight.

I'm in the forever corner;
and wishing.

Quetzalcoatl

Quetzalcoatl plumes
the frantic heavens
in the stars of his singing;
light, spilling ancient from
the eyes of his jet-far temple,
as He shakes the scarlet
from the desert blanch.
And He coils a comet tail
around our eyeful linger;
rutting the elixir of
our wholly quiet
as we wander the agave edge
of whale-split sea.
Under moon-high cicada,
we watch the Lording knight
in His very wrath
swallow the Milky Way
in one despotic bite.

And Quetzalcoatl,
the fiery mischief of
pinwheeled galaxy;
royal in His deep coat;
insinuates the breath
of nightful hands,
held opulent in all their
sins and sated drift;
raging the hunger
of curved evanescence
under the sudden eyes
of your culpable nakedness:
languidly,

ourselves enfold, under
the laughter of His shining fury;

only and only;
ever;
devoured delirious;
raining the drown
of pearlescent light:

the fire of you;
the splendid eyes of
my consuming.

Undark in these gliding sands
in summer-sudden night,
we hold the whispered fall
of limitless arms:

and Quetzalcoatl,

indigo thief of
always plumed heaven
pours forth the tantrum
of His midnight shards
and blandished light;
carelessly deepened
into heartward glances:
He quakes the roar of
our piercing wound
as we run the rings of
our drunken moonfall,

and kiss the burn of
undeniable honey.

Simple Words

Our sails lay sullen
in restful repose upon
a night wind
softer than the
sigh on your breast.

Casting a carefree leg
seaward, we lie
coiled casual on the deck;
shoulder to head,
hair entwined like
infatuated fingers.
Slowly we sway
in the eternal rocking
of sated senses
and longing ocean.

The simple words you
slide silken into
the whispered spaces
lying between us
harbor heartfelt fire.

Restlessly confessed

in the low tones
of a forlorn buoy,
they demurely drift
on the frailest fog of
ghostly hope.
And I am lost;

adrift in
the rest of forever;

letting go into
this deeper drowning
and the soulful chambers of
mermaids and sleeping moons;
awash in the shine
of losing myself
in this simple moment
of cascading confusion
and breathless holding.

Together,
finally pressed,
our reaching hearts abeam
through moon rings and
haloed magenta Milky Way…
into the starry tumble
of bluest midnight,

you and I;

your breast
removed from the sigh,
and the helm left
without hands.

A Dance Beneath Scars

Ethereal, your weave under night's scar;
a sliver of bone: insinuation
of linger in reticent eyes. A tear
in my soul, your gateway and retreat. Sin

laid to clover, we sway the darkened sound;
a unison of wounds rising to hope,
an escape of touch, so floatingly down,
where sapphire has eyes to dance, and provokes

our languid race of pulse; satin stained
and desire damned; whispered of scarlet winds.
Please, now, touch me where life has deeply laid
upon me; let me hear your truth spoken in

strange tongues; a fluency of fire and
rush, that pales the blood in our quickened moon;
a rumination of curve, warm pressed to hand;
oceans drowned against your draw, as you move

the jazz of you so deep upon my flame;
a silk slight falling; the breath of your name.

Window

I could hardly glance at you…

The sky has forgotten
to fall

upon my eyes,
fall in this light after
light;

which, against heaven

Junipers murmur
obsidian to white:
Pinon sleep a quiet lilt,
as quail tuck their dreams
whiskey away; and into
the collapse of peacefully
vermillion:

lies now calico into evening;
lies now diamond to wing

among the hands that
spill their blue upon
this covenant of candle
and canyon sway.
Breathes the night;

you have forgotten me…

A voice I can no longer hear

in this place where I have stood
and never walked;

ancient words,
windborne to cedar
I have stood with
heart to heart
in their ages;

epochs of soul, worn
sand smooth in
long whispers
that spill through mesquite
across the dark hearth
of desert time and
mesas patient in
white drift.

And into the rising,
still in the ancient tongue;
I set you

Morning Star

deep upon the darkly
glass; a flare;

you move through me,
dressed only in sky;
a reflection in frost;

an intimacy of breath
we have forgotten to hear;

and in this place where
you have walked, but never

stood;

an open hand tangles a stray
caress; moon to the touch;

an illumination;

phantom close among
lazily arms; and now

lies the quail, startled as sun;
lies the chestnut and curve;
lies the softly and burn

of light upon
eyes not forgotten
to

stars.

Canticle

Razor wire from vein,
we untangle them;
this contraband of shining
in the never-quiet mind;
these beautiful little deaths
we pull from our sleeve

voila!

appearances kept;
fallen kings and angels in red and black;
drifting dust down a garnet letting.

Because we do not talk;
Because we...

Have we ever, really;
you and I?

Voices rasped in shadow words of desert;
sinuous between ruined truths;
these half-shades of doors ajar;

> *voci nella ombri...*
> *voci che tagliano pietra...*
> *voci in seta sanguinante...*

O, what have I just said?

It little matters:
Everyone hears,
and hears
        nothing.

We do not talk;

We do not…

know how to cry.

And I am holding you because
these are the only hands I have;
and I gather you up
for these are the only arms I have.

Stillborn in the silent dry;

under a marionette moon,
I rattle, bones to heaven,
for this is the only husk I can frail.

With your eyes, show me
a lucid sky; diamonds that
only fall crimson to thorn;

place a kiss upon Cabot's ring;
back beaten, knees to stone:

palms open in the plead;

prayer by pain, unraveled;
cut upon the vision edge
of desire; for this is the only voice I have,
so I sing; I sing for
                    you;

and in the weep,
we

split the side to bleed the

dream.

Psalms

Levon wears his war wound like a crown...
I have done justice and righteousness;
do not let the arrogant oppress me...

In the blood of our autumn,
when the hour of calling
flies awash in cranes praying
the diminished cries of
recanting light across the dying moor;
I forged a psalm with the steel of my Fathers.
Prayer upon note, the hammer fell,
etched deep of crimson and cut
in the refinement of pyre.
In the faith of Their fervor
we wield the sword of Solomon
to sunder the petulant mother
from the ruined child;
taking sides in the perfect circle,
we bleed the requiem
from the alabaster rose.

Their throat is an open grave...

When the sorrow of thrush is
cloaked in the sweep of indigo bells
across the hushed hour
of our gathering slumber;
the touch of bronze
slowly fades into flowing fire:

the Thames, the Seine
Euphrates and Rhine;

the Oarsman's boat
so quickly shored
against the burning shoals.

The bones of my Children,
lost in the thorn of your meadow,
are scattered to shrike and dust
among the killing hedgerow;
disregarded and dealt low.
You have grieved your hour,
pound for pound;
and now, so uncried,
you are dried and done
and malignant on
your merry way.

> *Hold them guilty, O God…*

In the toss of midnight prayers,
when saints and lovers clutch the moon
in the eye of their trembles;
loft, she lies, lost in her lover's breast;
sojourned in the scarlet sound
of his sighs and the contraction
of rending hearts;
the soul of her breath spent
in the sweep of missing hands
across the sheets of her sorrow;
the wound that blooms eternal
in the garden of her mocking.
Among the clutter of nightstands,
their impatient dreams
gather dying dust.

> *Heed the sound of my cry…*

Unknown in the forgetful dust
of this falling place,
where death is the lesser fear:
afar in his drowning fire,

where heat is the following shadow
and cold is the honest companion:
cradled in acacia and smoke;
the ghost in the ghostly machine;
he draws winter, bullet by breath,
dying the distance of daughters
under the draining sky.
With hands stained of
cordite and brotherhood,
he holds the piece of his last self
worn weary to silver
and ragged remembrance:

    the flash of our wildfire;

    these strands of moon-shy pearl
    fluttered across the tapestry of
    of our coy fingers and
    topaz-brilliant linger;
    lacing the weave of dance
    awash in the dizzied haze
    of empty halls
    resplendent of furlong faces:
    confetti cartwheeled;
    jitterbug splendid;

    borealis

    you.

But that was another heaven,
another hope,
another me;

before creases ran
their rampage through
my forlorn memory.

I have failed,
my Wishful Splendor;

I have failed.

Forgive me the weight of silences
and the apologies of Christmas
and gathered tables.

Forever
across the gloaming hill
I will be the breath
of summer mischief
that beckons your waning eyes
to dance among
meteors and moons;
and find my final strength
to bear you up in the
moment of your turning time:

ever; and ever afar,
in reverent whispers; to

breathe the Psalm of your name

in irrevocable sun;
to gleam heaven,
earthward immortal,
and wash your
angel-bare shoulders
in delicious starlight.

I Turned

Imagining laughter
I turned

heartlong into a
beauty of
light clattered
nightfall,
bruised silken
by a deeply
hummingbird brushing...
whorled magnificent
into the eyeful
desires
of seraphim
skies
and ruby soothed
gold.

And I heavenly marveled

imagining
my only nightwardly
transfixed world
indecently sunward and
fire lavished
upon this Shiva-kissed
suddenly
grace;

I turned
from the sharded
meanderings
of my wavered life;

I turned

as everything
wind-torn tiredly will:
ash down and
mindfully echoed into the
emptier sense of my utter
unsleeping.

I have wasted my life
edging the run of horizons
from the farther chance
of openly living:
imagining clarity
across the cluttered page;
dying by degree,
into the rusting
degrees.

For I am the
spilling of words and
endless blood…
I am turning emptiness
enfolding forlorn
into this only sky that has
wiped my eyes golden
into a farther

hoping;

a dream unburdened of the
hopelessness I yet carry
in these languished arms:
to be, once more willing
to hold all the sadness
wept from every
angel burnished heaven:

willing me to carry
the heaviest of all burdens:

hope.

And I am oceans done.

I will never know poetry again:
I will never sing the stars
from their delightedly,
sleep drowned sea;

I will never know the moon
or the rumored pale it hushes onto
unsuspectfully dawdled,
foot-bare souls:

I cannot
understand these outside
the contexting Lux
of your fragrant, every

being.

I will ever,
only breathe
you.

I will only

(mattering little
to the very littleness
of a heart I hold in
my word-madly song spinning)

ever only hear your sounds
from a dove-turned
softly darkness,
in the facile any knowing I have;
my fractured
fumblings of just this
deafness of a
heart

and dancingly immaculate,
rose rained

yours:
with all the
burning

joyously

our honey mingled hands
can whisperingly away tease
from a sun tuliped vast,
and the nightingales of our
lily starred persistency,
kissed sapphire eternal

between.

Convenience Store Burritos

The sidewalks in Dallas were my favorite.

The ants there are compassionate, or at least their sting didn't penetrate my exhaustion. Not like Amarillo. Fuck. Those ants sting hotter than a Texas sun burns. No matter how sick, how delirious…how drunk, I never slept in Amarillo. Not a minute.

The first Warped Tour; 4 weeks in. August in Texas…I'm almost certain.

I'd been sick since June. Ear infections antibiotics couldn't touch. After the fires and the hottest, most humid summer in decades, my health was destroyed. I took this job as a last, dying hope. They called it a recession…but California's economy didn't recede…

It vanished.

It seemed like a good idea; up in a box seat at the Roxy, next to Don Johnson and some bit of fluff…severe make-up and tightly bulging dress. She looked almost 20. Talked on her cell phone through the entire Bob Dylan concert. He never looked at her. She was arm candy; nothing more. He was too excited about Bob Dylan to notice something like an actual person…and she obviously didn't give a shit about him. He was 5 years past being somebody. That's forever in Hollywood.

Me…I couldn't concentrate long enough to hear the music. My infections were worse at night…I had to work hard to take all of this in. Life is so fucking surreal when you're that sick.

So…whaddya think? Will you do it?

What the hell…why not? It's not really like I had a choice.

I was going to build the first mobile climbing wall and take it on tour around the country. A friend of mine who I put up first ascents with got the gig. He was no craftsman, though, and he needed me to actually build it. So I did. It was going be a real climbing wall…not like the cheesy things they have now. I already made hand holds and shipped them all over the world. I knew I could do this. The money they were offering was staggering, and I was so broke, anything sounded good.

It was a last chance to keep my life.

I finished the wall on a 105 degree day in Claremont. I passed out in the heat and smog. They found my body strewn among the metals studs; tool pouches spilling self-tapping screws and clamps. My father threw water on me and drove me home. I barely made it into the air conditioned house.

Get ready. We have to go to the engagement party.

I'm too sick to go, sweetie. You go. I need to stay home and rest.

This did not sit well. I guess I had been sick too often for her tastes and this particular engagement party was very important. Very. I barely knew the guy.

She, apparently, knew him very well.

He was an old boyfriend of hers from High School marrying some "bitch" from Georgia. The girl seemed nice to me, but what did I know? I only met her once, but she laughed easily and was beautiful in a way that only Southern women can be. She was delightful.

How can you be so selfish? I swear if you don't go to this I am through with you!

I looked at her in disbelief. She was standing on the staircase with a packed bag. I had a temperature of 102. I was so delirious I couldn't walk, let alone drive.

I showered up and went. I don't remember anything about the evening at all.

That seemed like a decade ago, here on the sidewalk in the "artistic" section of Dallas with the friendly ants. I tried to stand, but faltered. I looked drunk, but I honestly hadn't had anything to drink in over 2 hours. I was probably sober.

I looked at my watch, and then remembered. *Yeah, about that.* It went MIA in Houston. They don't have ants in Houston. My bus broke down and I had no place to go. By the time we got the wall taken down and packed away, all the spots were taken. I sat in an underground parking lot at the Astrodome and cried Somebody jacked the watch when I fell asleep. The lead singer of L7 finally took pity on me and put me on their bus. I slept on and off on the 8 hour drive to Dallas on the steps of their bus.

It didn't really matter what time it was. There wasn't going to be breakfast this morning. There wasn't enough money in the Tour for food anymore. We were sponsored by a micro brew, though, so there was always plenty of beer. Just no food.

I took out my wallet. At least that was still there. The two $100 bills that I had stashed away for emergencies had dwindled down to 7 quarters. The Promoters had missed every payday so far, and I was flat broke. I never made the dinner provided by the venues. I worked too long on the wall. The Tour couldn't afford enough roadies, so my partner and I did the work of 8 men by ourselves. Usually.

Angie Walton used to help. She of Daily Bread fame. When she wasn't flirting with Bradley of Sublime. That was during his "Clean" phase when he wasn't doing drugs or cheating on his wife, according to the biography on VH1. Would it be improper of me to say that they were smoking pot and fucking?

Probably.

Tony Hawk even helped once. I was blown away. He told me he was in awe of how brave climbers were.

I had a hard time digesting that.

I had just seen him deck off a 20 foot, back-side air. I mean, Tony Hawk missed the ramp entirely and hit the deck…and bounced back up in the air at least 3 feet. He broke 2 ribs and didn't skate for about a week.

He got back up and waved at the screaming fans. He wouldn't let anybody help him until he got inside the bus. It's the ethic of the skater: you ALWAYS get back up. No matter how much it hurts. I liked that. I adopted it as my own. And now I was standing here with this legend, an extreme sport hero, Tony Hawk, and he was telling me I was brave.

It was one of the proudest moments of my life.

I made my way down to a 7-Eleven. The air was cool inside, but the clerk was already looking at me crosswise. I got to the deli. The sandwiches were too much, and no matter how drunk I was, they always seemed a bit dicey.

That left Tina's Burritos.

A foot of pure lard and something brown and spicy not meant for human consumption. I felt safe with them, though, because you nuked them. Nothing could survive that. If you were lucky the clerk wouldn't notice you dumping nacho cheese on it as you left.

I had eaten a lot of these over the past month. I ate whatever gas stations and truck stops had to offer since I never made it to dinner on time. I'm sure that added to my deteriorating health.

I went to grab one and reality set in: $2.25. Fuck.

I walked outside. My stomach was howling. I leaned up against the stucco and collected myself as best I could.

Excuse me, can you spare 50 cents? I really need to eat.

I guess I looked pathetic enough. It only took twelve tries.

I walked back into the store. Felt the cool air on my skin. Smelled the stale coffee against the scent of cardboard. And there it was. Another meal.

I took out my wallet to get the final 7 quarters, and looked at the last thing in my wallet worth anything:

Brandee and Courtney in the backyard. Blissful. Digging a hole to China, Daddy, to China. Itty Bit with a plastic shovel and a wild-eyed smile on her face. Brandee with her favorite green dress on…the color her Daddy loved the most. Beautiful and happy.

I walked out and dropped the quarters into a payphone.

Hello. Larry is not here. He's gone right now. Larry, if this is you, I've taken the kids to my mothers. I'm leaving you.

Click

I walked back to the compassionate ants and laid back down. The sun was high in a burning sky. I didn't feel anything. I wasn't even hungry any more.

I tried to go back to sleep

if I could sleep,
if I could just sleep
if my eyes would close,
and my mind would stop
and I could really sleep

then this didn't happen, none of it

no…I wasn't sick

and I could get home
and my job would still be there
and my girls would be laughing in the backyard

and I would hold them
and smell the flowers of their impossibly soft hair and I would help them find China and…

I woke up among the ants.

I had a large bag of Doritos on my chest. And a post-it note on my access badge:

Larry, you look like you can use these more than we can. Hope things get better.

They actually took the time to look at my name.

I walked to the van and grabbed two pint bottles of Black Dog Ale and ate the Doritos for breakfast. The Tour always had plenty of beer, and I always wanted to be drunk.

I rubbed my eyes and walked slowly back into the heat and reality.

You always get back up.

Days Like These

for William Kuechlin

Under his gaze, everything becomes an impossibility.

The hook was a number 10, and my four-year-old fingers were having a tough time getting it to snell. They tangled and re-tangled and dropped in the fluster for the tenth time.

Son! What hell's wrong with you?

Nuthin' Dad...nuthin.

I knew I could do this...I had been practicing all summer. Today was different, though. Much different. The wind turned an impatient oar against the skiff. Mallards laughed their accusatory notions into my panic. I cringed against them. The air droned a buzz under my thoughts. Nothing in my mind was still today.

He was still looking at me...still looking...

Yes!

You did it wrong.
There are only five turns on that snell.
How many do we tie?

Six, Dad.

You're going to lose a fish and cost us dinner.

My first fishing trip. We hadn't caught a thing.

The cork handle of my Zebco 33 was still rough to the touch; too new to be worn smooth in such small hands. I loved that fishing pole. I practiced with it all summer long, and this was my reward: fishing with Dad and Grandpa K on a real boat. I pinned a red worm under the scowl at the stern,

turned my back and read the water
under a deep breath:

Two tree tops sticking out of the water.
Color is darker to the right; deeper water,
Grandpa sez, fish deeper water.

Just like home…

I swung the bait out of my hand and pitched it right into the cover. Just like pitching the sinker into a paper cup in the Backyard.

Nothing to it.

Heat was a murky sheen against the blue. The bait faded two feet out of sight…and the reel sang.

ting ting ting ting

A Zebco 33 sounds a little like a wounded school bell when the drag plays out line…and that fish was runnin' freight train away into the weeds.

Don't worry Larry…let him run.
They all come back if you give 'em room.

Grandpa had his hand on my shoulder,
and his eyes on my soul.
He stopped two feet shy of the weeds when I started taking back line.

Held my tongue just so.
Rod tip up…bow to him when he runs.
Take in the line when he stops to rest.
Don't bull him in.

I cranked right up to the surface as he popped out into the

sunlight. Glistening teal and gold. Easily a pound; probably more. Grandpa dropped his hand to my shoulder and gave me a squeeze.

> *Stupid Bluegill…they taste like crap.*
> *Throw him back and catch a good fish.*

I looked at my father just in time to see him turn his back.

I threw my Zebco 33 down, fish, line and all. Teal and gold splashed color onto the grey aluminum hull. It was the only fish we caught that day.

> *What is wrong with you, Larry?!?*

You might wonder how I can remember something that happened when I was only four and a half with such clarity.

Well…no matter how much dark you bury yourself in…or how many bottles you drown yourself in.; no matter how many prayers you say to keep that shadow tucked neatly into a childhood corner;

it just doesn't matter:

days like these never fade.

The journey started out from Escondido. Uncle Max. Old world German. Breakfast of eggs, bratwurst and zwieback. Aunt Susie (pronounced Soooo-sie) she gave you more food than 4 people can eat in one sitting. I can still taste those zwieback biscuits.

Damn.

And my first cup of coffee
very sweet and lots of cream.
Just like Grandpa.
I still drink it just that way.

Laughter and meals

sounds of old world family.
Life and love

the way it was before the wars that drove my family here to the
United States. Smiles and happiness my family did not know when
they were afraid to admit they were German.

My great grandfather Kuechlin changed the spelling of our name
to make it look more American.

He wanted to fit in.

I loved my Uncle Max immediately. Like an older version of my
Grandpa K, but with a heavier accent. My Grandpa and Max were
natural salesman. Everybody loved them right away; and came
back because they were real people, people who loved with
abandon, and didn't bother with consequences.

Grandpa…William Kuechlin…Bill, ran the most popular
gas station in San Pedro.

A port town; blue collar tough.
People who made their living
with their hands
on the wharfs and in the factories.

Real people living real life.

He ran a Union Oil station; 76. On San Pedro Avenue near
Wilmington Avenue, across from Banning High.

It is still there.

Max and Grandpa hugged their brotherhood and laughed their
goodbyes as we walked out into the half light of burgeoning day.

We packed into the Ford Fairlane 500 and took off for Lake
Henshaw, a mud hole of a lake in the mountains east of San
Diego. The road to Henshaw…Highway 78…was a two lane
twister through the scrub oak and Manzanita. I sat in the back

seat with my thoughts…sliding to and fro on the blood red vinyl;
the direction based on the curve and the weight of the foot placed
on the Fords pedal.
I thought back to everything I had been taught:

all the lessons my father had given me
and the tips my grandfather had taught me.
I wanted to do this

right.

And I wanted to catch the biggest fish.

In the Kuechlin family, there was no other outcome: we
always catch the biggest fish.

We never go away empty handed. Never.

Nervous talk with Grandpa.
Laughing for no reason.

Singing the old songs
the ones his grandma taught him
German songs of life in the wheat
songs of loving life with old hearts
songs of winters I never knew.

Laughing and laughing

and silly talk between
two hearts connected by life

and the Chevy Bel Air passed us so fast…
the Ford pushed hard to the right.

Around the blind corner;
my eyes can see this

I can see

paper plates billowing
in the perfect morning blue
perfect white against the stone walls
perfect incision of metal and stone

and I can see

I can see

these young eyes
I can see the Ford slowing
see men tumbling blind
see glass and fire
see blood and
see men falling out
see a man holding an eye
back into his head with ruined hands
see a man bleeding from his ears

and

falling

falling

and below
below the man shaking in the dirt
below the flames in morning blue
below the window
below my door
with these young eyes

I see

below the door
the ends of glass and cut

torn cloth

and so much blood

and his face;
turned to meet
his life
his warmth

his memories and meaning

leaving

leaving

leaving him in rhythm with
a heart that refuses to forget.

His eyes were crimson closed by the time his heart
caught up to the memory.

And I was four years to heaven.

We dazed away to call for help.

That's what's wrong, Dad.

    You saw what?

Promise.

No! You did not, son. You did not see that.
Stop it, young man! Quit being stupid.

I saw it too, Larry. I saw him there. We both saw him.

My Father just stared at my Grandpa. He started the boat and
guided it back to the dock. We left for home in silence.

Five days later I jumped off the bus from school and saw a
familiar sight: a teal blue Corvair parked across the street from my
house. I ran in to give my Grandpa a huge hug.

Come on, Larry. I want to take you somewhere. Grab the Zebco.

We drove PCH down to the coast; laughed quietly; my Grandpa teasing me and tickling me and making me laugh. I remember laughing because I never wanted to laugh.

I didn't want to laugh.

We parked in Sunset Beach, near the water tower. Grandpa took me down to the water's edge in Anaheim Bay, and the tide was running in

turning the Eel Grass into the drowning sun
heard the cranes across the long flats
raucous in their meals
heard the splash of fish in the currents.
Heard the Mergansers heading off into night
heard the long call of surf across the shore.
Saw the gold of afternoon
felt it pulling me into quietly black.
Felt the night softly on my eyes.

See him there, Larry…see his fins?
There in the dark water.

I made the cast and caught my first Corbina. Grandpa said he was really big. Took him home for dinner.

We sat in the rushes, there in the breath of darkness
in the light that has forgotten its flame
watched the cranes work into darkness;
whispers of white against deep umber.
You don't forget days like these.
My Grandpa with his arm around me.
A day fading in the hush.

I don't remember going home.

Crazy Walking Dude

I had a friend named Danny.

Nobody called him that, except me. The rest of the town called him Crazy Walking Dude because of the too-large strides he used to tear through town, and the way he rocked wildly side-to-side,

always with a face serious as sin.

He had a full-length coat that he wore every day of the year that was hand-stitched from other articles of clothing. That's all he ever wore on his back. I never saw him wear a shirt underneath, even in winter.

He lived in a cave out on the Sunset Cliffs. I was always jealous of his digs; he had the best view on the Point.

He was the icon of our community, like the famous Spaceman Bill before him. Ocean Beach took good care of him, but nobody talked to him. They were afraid to. And he stayed to himself, mostly.

Me…I talk to everybody.

We became friends in the alley. I used to see him in the morning, up even earlier than I usually get up, walking the alleys, grabbing the cream off the "Ocean Beach Recycling System"…anything useful that's left over from the dozens of moves per day. We leave these treasures in the alley so they can find a good home. I used to save the best stuff for Danny, sometimes throwing them in the back of my truck so I could give them to him the next morning.

I'm sitting on one of those items as I write this.

It started as a nod. Nothing more.

He wore his malady like his coat: his thoughts stitched together and tattered. The, there was the slightest of waves. Every morning, a nod and a wave. Weeks passed this way. Finally, when he found himself cornered one morning, I asked him his name. He answered in a steady name as he strode off:

My name is Danny

    My name is Larry! I answered back over his shoulder.

A few weeks later, I was walking the Sunset Cliffs with a friend after a session at Abs. John and I were deep into the BS of our "great rides" and needling each other about our pratfalls. It's a narrow trail with lots of cover. As we came into a small clearing, I was suddenly fact to face with my alley friend.

    Danny! How are you?

Hey, Larry... As he strode off.

It was the only time I ever saw him smile.

Three days later, I drove the back way into town to do some work in my office, and had to stop for some jumbled traffic. It's a road that locals use…no stoplights.

POP….POP POP POP…POP POP… POP POP

I jumped out of the truck to see what happened. People were running everywhere. Two policemen had stopped Danny on his way back from the liquor store. They shot him when he dropped the 40 he held in his raised hands.

POP

They were intent on disarming him…taking the only tool he owned: a Buck knife, dull as the May morning he laid in.

An angry crowd gathered loudly and quick. Ocean Beach was furious. The two cops, eyes dilated and dark, brandished their 9's and waved the crowd away:

and ebb and flow of anger and fear.

> *Get back!*

You fucking shot him!

Somebody call an ambulance!!
Where's the goddamn ambulance?!

> *Get back! BACK!*

I ignored the guns and din. I could only watch my friend writhe on the street and clutch his coat.

Eight rounds in the upper torso.
A tight pattern. 2400 foot pounds.

But Danny was defiant and strong. He lived in the real California, deep in the red earth of our Cliffs. He was forged of a life that we no longer remember, and could no longer survive.

It took him a long time to die.

He didn't cry out. He just took in the sky and clutched the pride in his coat.

I watched his life run the long drain out to the sea.

Ocean Beach has never been the same. We no longer have an icon; a physical statement of our protest and defiance. Our souls cannot bear it; the cops won't allow it and we won't stand up to them. We no longer have the heart to. It died on the corner of Voltaire and Bacon:

8 rounds for a 40 ounce offense.

www.ingramcontent.com/pod-product-compliance
Lightning Source LLC
Chambersburg PA
CBHW060817050426
42449CB00008B/1704